AF441398

Missouri Poets and Poetry Series Prrsents:

The State of Affairs

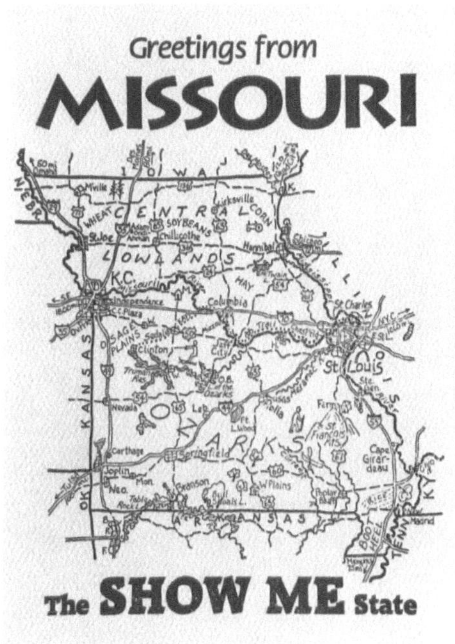

Edited by Jason Ryberg

Spartan Press
Kansas City, Missouri
spartanpresskc,com

Cover image: From "The Social History of the State of
    Missouri" by Thomas Hart Benton.
Author photos: Riley Kemper, Bob Elliot, Agnes Vojta,
    Dane Marti, Bonnie Close, Rich O'Donnell

Acknowledgments:

Special thanks to the Osage Arts Community, Mark McClane, Matt McClane, Tony Hayden

The authors would like to thank the editors of the following publications where some of these poems (in one form or another) were formerly published:

Ken Gierke: "Freddie Freeloader," "One Last Door:" *LatinosUSA*, "Don't Lose Heart:" *SHINE Poetry*,"Sikeston to Memphis:" *Trailer Park Quarterly*, "Have a Safe Flight:" *The Rye Whiskey Review*, "Treading Water:" *Rusty Truck*

Anna Lum: "The Edge:" *Webster Review*, *Celery Flies* (Moonshadow Press) "Sitting Down for Yourself:" *Crossing the Divide*, *Celery Flies* (Moonshadow Press).

Clarence Wolfshohl: "Fruits of Innocence:" *All roads lead home*, "Looking at Hammersmith Bridge . . ." *Rattlesnake Review*.

Scot Young: "johnny cash blues:" *Because Nothing Can Be Saved*, "and those who can, teach," "haiku sonnet: child protective services:" *American Haiku*, "boys of summer," "first gig:" *All Around Cowboy*

Table of Contents:

Sharon SingingMoon

Clarence Wolfshohl

"Don't get me lying to you:" A phrase used to start a story, indicating they will tell the truth, often heard in southeast Missouri.

-Google

Walter Bargen

Walter Bargen has published 29 books of poetry. Recent books include: *Days Like This Are Necessary: New & Selected Poems* (2009) and *Trouble Behind Glass Doors* (2013), and *Too Quick for the Living* (2017). *My Other Mother's Red Mercedes* (2018), *Pole Dancing in the Night Club of God* (2020), and *Orwell at the Kremlin* (2024). His awards include: a National Endowment for the Arts Fellowship and the William Rockhill Nelson Award. He was appointed the first poet laureate of Missouri (2008-2009). www.walterbargen.com

Dull Night Toward Salvation

The woman with the crowning oak tree
tattooed in dendritic detail
on the back of her neck,

roots rising up from her shoulders that twist and knot
into braided hair as she moves between tables,
brown t-shirt and holey jeans, topping off half-empty

coffee cups, taking late-night orders.
The bulbed back of her shaved head,
a blank billboard over tangled shadows

of stricken branches. Customers
intent on reading their cup-stained bottoms,
the prophetic limits of their late lives.

Above Formica-topped tables,
steam-licked windows wait to be rewritten.
This late ending looks closely

at what lies out there: streetscape, fire escape,
escape, a tree on the back of a woman's neck
that must sometime drop its leaves.

The Late '60s On Her Fiftieth Birthday

He's waiting for his wife to eat the mushrooms.
It's not something he's cooked and serves on a plate,
but pulled from a small plastic Zip-loc bag
that sat decades in the back of the freezer. He's not sure
if he should say *drop* or *down* or *eat please*.

The dogs must be walked.
Who is to be leashed is in question.
She's off down the driveway, past the persimmon grove,
leaves dropped, a few fleshy, wrinkled, testicular fruit
hanging from arthritic branches

She stoops, cautious of her injured back,
picking up fallen persimmons, spitting seeds
as she walks, as if she enters the forest
leaving a trail of seeds to find her way back,
a path that will take decades to grow.

The Art of Loving

Lying on the creaky wooden floor,
dust covered, something I'd read fifty years ago,
left heavily underlined, before I realized
relationships don't make sense, it's something
we do to each other. Anyway a cat had pissed on it.

Not a big surprise, beyond purring, the cat often
comments directly, curling up on the page I'm reading,
or shredding the poem I'm writing,
and now abandoned on the desk, perhaps preferring
different more abrupt line breaks.

Rarely is the cat this dismissive.
What was I to do but throw the reeking book
onto the porch where a day later
it is covered with eighteen inches of snow
that smoothed out all the scars and the rutted road,

blankly outlining the silence of every branch
and page. The snow shovel uncovered the book,
an inch of ice replaced the missing cover,
hermetically sealing what would never get out
to make sense of this world.

Back from the Aquarium

At the automatic sliding glass doors,
exit to the yellow lines of an asphalt sea
where the latest metallic species shimmer,
giant enameled jellyfish that float out to the road
on the latest climate driven flood, except his pickup
truck that's sinking to the rusty bottom, snagged
by a concrete parking barrier.

Yes, he knows this man but not in this state,
though it is late in both their lives,
and there's no driving out of the waves
where they find themselves marooned,
the salty crest unreachable. Treading deeper
is all they can do together. There is a gray mist

on the black seas face where Neptune sharpens his
trident. They stare at each other's apparitions.
In shorts and untied boots, wearing four layers:
unbuttoned shirt that lists toward his right shoulder,
a fast current drags his work boots along;
a canvas jacket marred by roadside flotsam

where he last capsized, dreaming
and forgetting; and a scarf that snakes
around his neck, not to be entangled
in the wake behind his blackened left leg,
the right blushes red, one calve
larger than the other after

crossing-the-median, the wreck that still swerves
through his lame stride. When they are through
with the "How are things going?" he circles his truck,
"At least you're on the right side of green."
The other man says, "I don't play golf," as he half-swings-
half-lifts one leg at a time into the truck's gaping maw.

Preponderance at the Front Door

1

Exhaustion so total his mind and body stop arguing.
He watches as they separate and walk off into
    different rooms.

No, his clothes aren't torn and shredded.
No scratches or bruises visible anywhere but on
    the walls.

More like friends who argued over who's the best
baseball pitcher, who serves the best beer, has the
    best car,

who has the worst friend. Mind and body shrug and
    don't look back.
Left alone, he wonders what's left, what's right, though
    the wandering is clear.

What's left of left? The distance grows quickly.
    To chase one is to sacrifice
the other, a hobbled celebration of self-negation.

Can he mediate, make a convincing argument to hang
    around,
If not together? Who should get the dog with her
    yapping desperation?

Perhaps a leash, a short lead, but to what end?
No answers. He just wonders in the wandering.

He's left with all the rest, though there isn't anyone else
    around.
What's left after the mind is lost and still conspiring.

2

The next trick of paltry remembrance, inevitable
    revisions,
listening to the can clank and roll as the body continues
    down the road.

No real destination in mind, perhaps a cliche, a warm
    beach,
crossing a pale desert's evening pastels.

Or this dirty street. What's left feels abandoned,
what can't rise up is suspended.

Defying gravity, a soul swings in the breeze.
Exhaustion still panting. Everything still out of reach.

Road Kill in the Study

1

Leave it blank that would be safest
by some measures, hardest by others.
Braking, the car spins out of control.
Crusted snow crushes and snaps with each step.
Ice hints at what is below.
The slash of pointed grass blades
still green this late in the season.
Withered frozen fingers of leaves.
What's slouching in the twisted wreckage
doesn't melt.

Erasers can't save the wounded, the mistakes
    irreversible,
irreparable. The wrong turns, stabs in the dark
that come back bloody, the back-tracking alley,
a dead end, forest too deep to cross--
all the hoped-for corrections, and after a while their
    fleshy
firmness wears out, leaving soft trails of rot
to follow, to reconstruct the stench at the page's edge.

2

Say nothing, that would be easiest,
by some measures, impossible by others.
Baseball bat and gun fall on both sides

of the street but the shores of the Rubicon
are not always so clear even if there are
birds chirping in the trees and bushes. Anyway,
it would most likely be Perche or Cedar Creek,
tributaries of no great consequence but where lifetimes
are expressed, exposed, and lost, time only a glimpse.
Find a distraction, an exercise, an illusion,
only another breath keeps us believing.

3

The road not taken, a dream, a nonexistent
realm. The same for the road taken.
There's no turning around as he is shoved along.
He doesn't bother to look back over his shoulder.
What's ahead is all he can and usually can't handle.
Barrel and bayonet more than is needed
to encourage his stumbling, progress not possible,
any respite a desperate forgetting,
a profound denial, depending on the rate of breathing,
flooded ditches choked for another withering hour.

Prophetic Detail

Saturday evening an ice storm savages the trees,
    a rabid animal
lashing out at the dark. Followed by an inch or so
    of snow
to bandage the ravaged and broken. No reason
    immediate enough,
demanding enough, urgent enough to go anywhere
    now or tomorrow.
The car parked below the iced white pines
where one heavy branch lies frozen to the car's trunk.

Monday morning, late, later than usual after cat care,
    breakfast, tending
to the wood stove, the usual reluctance and doubt at
    every turn, the wind cruel,
gusting 15 to 20 mph, I walk toward the car.
    Somewhere I see a long line
of long-coated, starving prisoners hollowing out a
    blizzard they follow back
to camp. I have this vision every winter, that is, when
    there is a winter.

Frigid dawn, all that needs to be done is open the car
    door, break the ice that's sealed it closed.
Wedge the ice scrapper into the widening crack and
    pry, and at the last moment pull

the handle that snaps and is instantly reduced to a
    meaningless piece of cheap
black plastic, not meaningless, dysfunction and failure,
    but useless. The options,
the passenger side door frozen more solidly shut. No
    Ali Baba wanting sesame chicken for lunch.

This late morning, flat bar in hand, the rear driver's side
    passenger door pried, opens,
the front seat folded forward, the front door shouldered
    open. Engine started,
the four-feet long crack along the bottom of the
    windshield begins to chirp,
the defrost on high, the temperature gradient too great
    between inside and outside.
Defrost shut off, a small hole worked in the windshield
    ice and I'm driving
neck craning as if a child on tiptoe to see the steaming
    peach pie on the counter.

Making a left turn onto the freeway entrance ramp,
The passenger side front door flies open as if hinged
    flight was a beginning
and the mail stacked on the seat lifts, a startled flock of
    bills that now perch
in the snowy weeds on the road's shoulder and the soot-
    stained pavement.
Envelopes in hand, I close the door that won't now stay
    closed,

the lock frozen in the unlock position. Belt looped
    through the arm rest,
I drive holding it closed, and even if Abraham's goat
    appears,
it's too late, the sacrifice done, the bloody steering
    wheel returned to the road.

Reporting Larceny

His uniform too dark to be blue, unless true blue
Disappears into darkness, and not autumn blue
But a blue welded to a night that has lost
Its sun and has us building megaliths, making blood
Sacrifices to pour over stones and into ditches,
Begging for light, any flicker, any thin arc.

The blue of retribution, vengeance,
Of injustice meted out, sometimes the knife
Pulled away from the throat and not across it,
If he's quick enough. Black belt holding
His holstered pistol, a radio transmitter
Strapped across his chest so he only needs to turn
His head to speak as if carrying on a lonely
Conversation with his shoulder.

Action compressed into the bulk of his body.
But for now, I sit next to his desk, writing a list
On the back of a discarded piece of paper like a small
Child ready to be reprimanded for being careless.
The time unknown except it must have been dark,
The day uncertain, even the week, but recently enough
To report. I thought it was theft but the policeman
Says larceny. At the top of the list is a hotchpotch
Of golf clubs and a golf bag because they were nearest
The door. They couldn't make it onto the green
With this set of clubs. Left behind is the hand-drawn,

cardinal red,
Collapsible cart. Perhaps renting a motorized golf cart
Was always the plan.   Surely of no use, my father's
Wooden-wheeled roller skates Circa 1935, and even
The three baseball gloves: One a very stiff catcher's
      mitt,
The other two fielders' gloves, one embossed with
      the signature
Of Bob Turley. Who was he? But what about the boy
      who wore
Those gloves each spring and summer for years,
His hand buried deep in their leather: running
Across the infield to catch the ball, make the out,
Swing the bat, get the hit, but always just wanting
To step out of the ballpark lights and go home,
Caught, suspended, in his father's dream.

A half-dozen deeply worn tools,
That belonged to my grandfather,
Maybe even older, nothing useable,
Nothing worth the carrying away
Except by memory. But the ornate tin
Cookie box, not very old, filled with personal
Papers that still needed to be sorted.
This is how I fail my parents again. The padlock cut
and gone, nothing recoverable.
The policeman hands me his card
With a case number on the back
And instructs me to call him if anything develops.

Cat's Play

He leaves her lying on the sidewalk outside the house.

She's not dead, not beaten, not sick
or destitute, not yet though these are stories
she tells herself. She's sleeping, or she was until
he said he was leaving. No, not forever

though the house he visits in town will be
all he remembers when he returns. She will be
sleeping again, this time in bed with the fan set on a
    chair
propelling itself no great distance. He recalls

the light of his leaving: long, yellow, elastic,
stretching until it snaps into darkness
at the edges of fields, along fences, between the blades
of brittle grass that edge the concrete, and in her voice
as she acknowledges his passing. He bends down
to kiss her on the forehead. She does not kiss
back. They watch a gray tabby chase its tail.
Think cute. They are no different:
staying, she leaves; leaving, he stays.

Gong World

From the local Alzhelimers Association I receive
the tip of the day,
On their own they walk into other rooms or down
the street to the new cafe
Without saying good-bye or leaving a tip,
As if the world rested flat on their faces and not on
my sore shoulders.

I've only heard rumors of and really don't believe,
and this points
To how far we have to go to cross the fence to
enter into the far field
To tip over a sleeping cow, as if an angus or holstein
wouldn't wake
with all the commotion of creaking fence posts and
barbed wire, ripping shirt sleeves.

The uncontrollable laughter of just how ludicrous
any of us can be
in our pointless mayhem. Yet the tip of the day is
clearly here:
"Yesterday is gong and tomorrow is uncertain."
I know the feeling,
I've played that music long ago and still do.

Nothing as delicate as Balinese gamelans, their chiming
    waterfalls leading
To the place we'd forgotten, that we once knew and in
    listening
Know again, where beginnings keep flowing and falling
To glow beyond in the clear water of it all.

Nothing so brash as the monstrous gong announcing
    the beheading
Or the benighted, or the daytime game show that sends
    the fool
On his way which is one way and no way. Lao Tse wrote
That in silence there is strength even as the world is
    going gong.

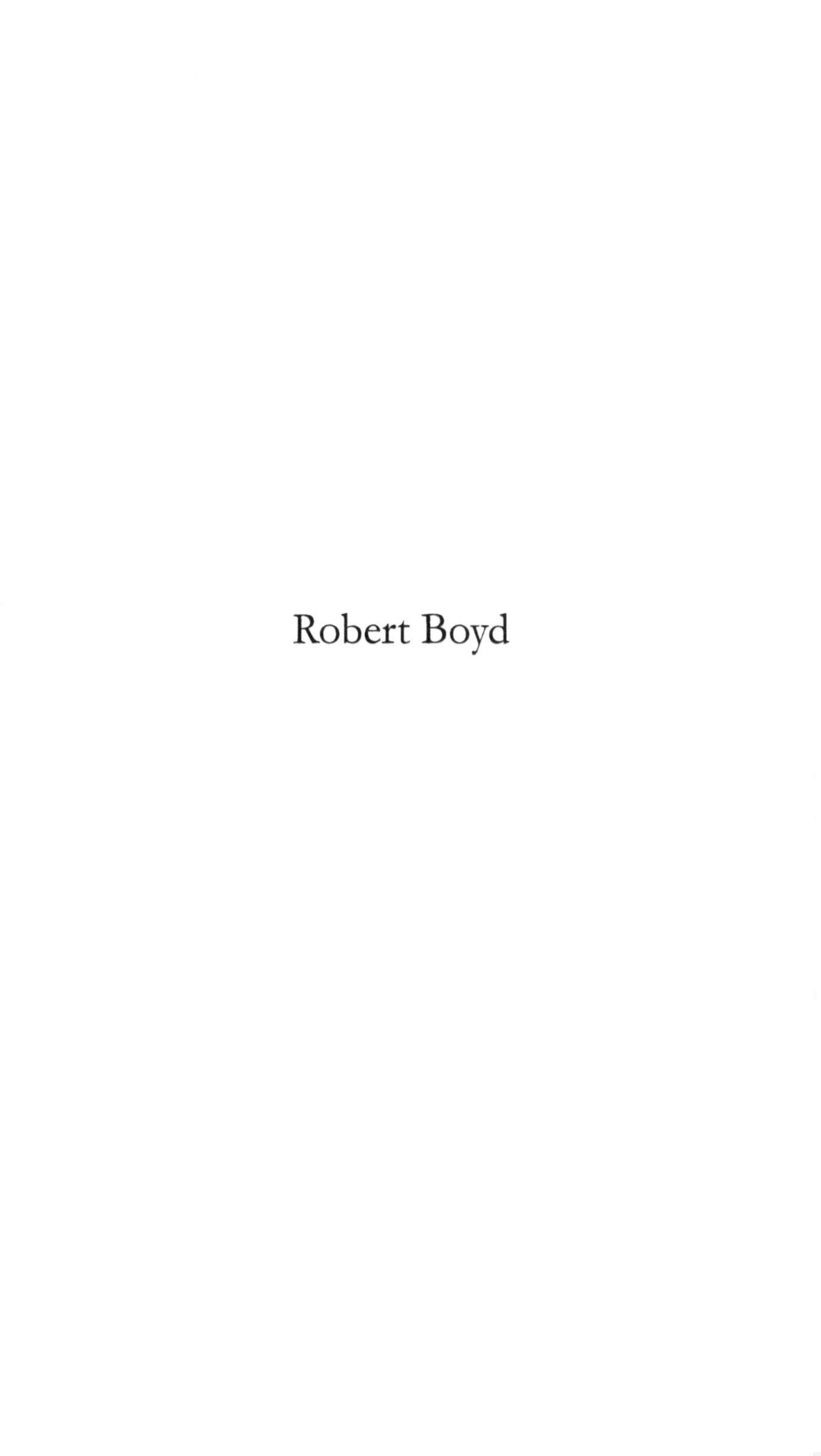

Robert Boyd

Robert Boyd is a retired teacher and free-lance journalist whose work has appeared in *The Nation*, the Chicago Tribune, the Los Angeles Times, and regularly from 1968 through the 1990s in the *St. Louis Post-Dispatch*. His stories and poems have appeared in *Southern Poetry Review*, *Confrontation*, *The Greensboro Review*, *River Styx*, *Webster Review*, *Chariton Review*, and elsewhere. He has won the Guy Owen Prize and the Missouri Writers' Week award for poetry. His novel, *Cohea's Tower*, and a book of his stories, *Family Values*, have been published by Yettie Publishing, St. Louis.

SNAPSHOTS FROM MY FAMILY ALBUM:
4. Swimming in Lake Catherine, about 1950

Sometimes a picture misses the important things.
You see the water, low, the bank of weeds pressed down,
Dry mud below it, and the bare bright wood
Of dock and diving board in stark noon light.
Hot weather, then; yet still this photo missed
The weight of thick mid-August Southern air
Wet as the stock-still standing lake itself.
Nor could it show the rancor baked into
The studied poses of these awkward boys
Waiting for girls who just don't seem to come
In time to catch their act. Yes, that is me,
There on the left, my brother by the rail,
Our cousin clowning on the diving board.
Don't let the smiles confuse you; we are ripe
For riot, set to go to foreign wars
With pleasure if that means we can escape
This inert countryside, this Southern grave
Of listless water and unyielding sun
Where there's no end to what cannot be done.

Snapshots From My Family Album:
19. My Children in mid-December, 1985

This is the old house, and its living room
Of paneled walls, tall windows opening
Upon wide yard and wider woods beyond
All white with rare December snow, where elms
Raise up their thin black arms in mock surprise.
Among them scattered junipers, as round
As spools of warm green yarn. It's one of these
That stands now in the corner of this room.
The children, having covered it with chains
Of paper, lights, and bright glass ornaments
Repose like heroes on the couch and floor.
They've left to me the angel that must go
On top of everything, where only I
Can reach; except for that small, vital task
I am irrelevant. This ample room
Gives all they need of walls against the cold
That peers in darkly from the winter woods;
The tree gives all they need of saving grace.
They do not think of what it takes to keep
The wan world outside while they watch or sleep.

Four Elements

1: Earth Rejects the Early Plow

I have a headache. Iron's
Too cold. It scratches, like my nerves
Are being pulled out. All they want
Is to get it in and over with.
Their idea of foreplay is dance
Or sacrifice, as if the blood
Of lambs or virgins, or the spilled wine
Lubricates.

But let them stay awhile; they know
My turnings and my shifts of weight
And how in time my dreams will drift
Toward flowers opening and wet
Life working into cracks in stone.

Soon, soon, I'll want to stir myself
And it will tap my bones,
The old sweet current, and I'll stretch
And swell toward their feet, wide-spread
To plow and sunshine.

It's like a hunger when it comes on me,
An appetite for folding in.
They know I can be hard as flint
Or round and full of nourishment, like fruit,
But when the season comes

Then I am hollowed with a space
Shaped like a seed
That needs the thrust of planting to be whole.

2: The Wind's Confession

Your life is crazed like a chapel window
Telling an allegory, now obscured

Hard to say whether from age alone
Or whether something struck it from outside

Listen: I can get my fingers into cracks
Smaller than you can measure to repair

That's why you feel a draft
For all the rags of doctrine here and there

Wrapped in your gown and headgear
On the ancient altar, your skin

Ruddy in the fire of the sacrament,
Pay attention to the pricking of your thumbs

That will be me, inside already,
Making good my promise . . . .

The music of my passing
Is cold, like plainsong. You should know:

I can lift you toward the splintered light
And I can let you go.

3: Fire, the Old Reprobate, Caught Red-handed, Cops a Plea

I have annealed and pasteurized
Cooked, lit, and rendered, carried goods
And put your footprints on the moon.

If I bring loss to some,
Or suffering,
Why, I do it without spite,
With perfect equanimity.

The plan of God
Who spoke me into blaze
And wielded me in vengeance
And cast me down alike
Upon the heads of saints
And liars, whores and kings
Is all I need of pretext
And ample mitigation.

Think of the ancient piñon pines,
Those noblest of hangers-on,
No good without me; their seed must couch
In virgin cones and cannot root
Until I ease them open with my tongue.

4: Water, Having Found Her Own Level, Sulking

I have been a traveler
In high places, higher
Than airplanes go, so high
That everything above is black
And what's below
Blues into hazy nothing,

And I have loved to fall
And flow and billow vaporous
And spin down to delicious drifts
Always working my way under
Deep, where thaw is
And the Heraclitan fire,
Toward beginning.

These days,
You see so little rise in anything. Dim sun
Can't lift the ice,
My currents, slowed by something, sink
And burrow in the deep mud,
Barely throbbing.

Only
At times I think back
To times of tidal surge and
Flooded streams, and long
For the feel of those

Distant parts of me gone out
Like offspring, gone to work
On all that's elevated, all that's rough
Stretched to the outer edge of touch
Just turning to come home.

Hunting With My Father In The Snow

Night seeps from the woods across the fallow ground
We've had enough of cold
The whisky warmth can't hold the winter back

Slowly he stands, his weight on me
This is a drill. We break the guns
We stow the spent shells in our vests

Across the field toward the hedge we walk in line
The dogs dance round us, belling the iron air
Our boots crack the brittle tufts of grass

He gestures; I look up, then down
It is that scene from Breughel
Below the valley is already dark
The sunset paints the woods above
Lights burn yellow in the cottage windows
Woodsmoke rises from the chimney pots

His broad form masks the path ahead
I need not look beyond him
The rabbits swing across his back
Their dead eyes glisten in the fading light.

A Letter to My Children For Valentine's Day

Mid-winter, and a sadness sags my bones
And slows my heart, and will not go away.

Strait as the stony path to heaven's gate
The narrow days dawn, dangerous with ice,
Which warns: look to this moment, nothing more.

Do you remember Thaïs, who converts
To Massenet's sweet music
Drawing life around her down to holy symmetry
And sweet remorse?

                I sit, bewildered, full
Of choices made and doubted, all those dull
Decisions heaped on duller ones, and know

The rising sun can light me nothing new,
And all that changes will remain the same.

I wonder how one makes a choice that leads
So far, through winter wilderness,
And toward what distant mountains one might go
To find respite.

                              Please forgive
This self-abuse. The next time I write
I will send you a bracelet
Made of polished stones that
Glitter in the warming sun.

Letters to My Children

On the State of The Farm in Fall

October, and our pond's gone up in flames
Once more an Autumn blaze of mirrored sumac,
    maple, elm
Dancing on the ripples in the wind

The green purse of our valley holds it in
Or else its fire would spill down field and track
And set the lower world alight.

The very birds, I swear, who kindled it last year
Choir in those trees around the lake
Like boys at barn fires, laughing and afraid

Beyond the dazzling hills, the winter clouds
Low, flat, and gray, are gathering;
They'll quench the conflagration in due time.

Now therefore come and sit with me
In your imagination, as I like to think
We did when you were young,

To pitch some pebbles in the pond
And watch the gold flames shatter and re-form
And talk, like migrant birds who've paused
To rest up for the next leg of their flight,
Of where we've been and where we've yet to go.

The Winnipeg Whore

                    -- Anonymous

When my dead father drank he sang this song, and so
    do I
I beat on his guitar and rage against the light;
His song is the tag of a film on a reel still turning
Whipping my brain; I take that for a metronome.
Tap your foot he told me once, you got no rhythm.
After he watched me through sixteen bars he told me
    never mind
And got a stick and beat time on my leg --

I still can't do without some sound advice.

We hung around water; he saw the world in flux
And held that vengeance rains alike on saints and dogs.
Was no ascetic, wolfed his beer from quarts,
Plucked trout from mountain streams without a qualm,
Dined on the sweet flesh of them fresh caught
Pan broiled, washed down with zinfandel,
Loved travel and the steady roll of ships
And the moment of the sun's sinking; there's a
    photograph
Two nuns on the S.S. Rotterdam in nineteen fifty-six

The sun just gone and afterglow lighting their white
     caps
Like alps; ah, he was fond of that. Now here, he said,
Think of the shame of snow and of these wintry nuns
Their heads encased in ice, their bodies nullified by
     black.

Drunk, he sang to melt all women's hearts, to chafe
     their thighs
With urgent words; he wanted juice to flow;
I think he meant to lap it up.

Now water gets to him by seeping down, and I'm left
     out
To play songs by myself and speculate
About the way things wash and flow and surge
And whether women of a certain kind still know
How to keep men warm in Northern parts.

Victor Clevenger

Victor Clevenger spends his days in a Madhouse and his nights creating art. He is a poet, collage artist, and small press publisher living in Carrollton, MO. Selected pieces of his work have appeared in print magazines and journals around the world. He is the author of several collections of poetry including *47 Poems* (Crisis Chronicles Press, 2022), *Every Angel in Heaven is a Hopscotch Champion* (Spartan Press, 2024), and *Slow Grinding* (Between Shadows Press, 2025). He can be reached at: crownofcrows@yahoo.com

Procrastination

i've written nothing since that week i wrote the
poems for slow grinding   i tried to write a
couple of weeks ago when i had a sudden urge
to capture the beauty of a birdsong & it all ended
up being more bunk than blue jay   more
mouthful of marbles than meadowlark   more
downed deadwood than a dickcissel so i gave up
& let the urge fly   but today at the madhouse i
overhead someone quoting maya angelou   *do
your best until you know better   then when
you know better   do better*   & that made
sense to me   maybe tomorrow i'll revisit bart's
dusty pigeons for inspiration & try once again
but tonight i'm busy watching the cat sleep
busy watching the cactus grow   busy listening
for water to boil   & busy wondering what the
hell happened to that seaborn jones book that
mike james loved so much

       in my lifetime
       all the circle paths i've walked
       going nowhere

Going Nowhere

repetitive rubbing   how long before the stone
becomes sand   before the sand becomes dust
how long is the duration of an hourglass flipped
over & then flipped & then flipped again   do
you trust time   do you feel like it is on your
side   is it of the essence
will only it
tell

       choosing to just wait
       for something better to come…
       boundlessly bound

Boundlessly Bound

she shares a bob marley quote she once heard &
enjoys   *some people are so poor all they have*
is money   i reciprocate with one from gandhi
you can't shake hands with a closed fist   it's
10:46 a.m.   it's tuesday   it's fourteen minutes
until the next work meeting starts   my younger
self might have tried try to convince you
otherwise   but i assure you
my life doesn't always
suck

> before the buzz died…
> a young coyote howling
> across the canyon

Before The Buzz Died

glass animals   gooey   tangled in the willows
now our tongues are tied   this old bed of rusty
nails gets softer & softer   bob kaufman once
wrote the radio is teaching my goldfish jujitsu
this afternoon the radio is reteaching us
to make love loudly with
the bedroom door
open wide

    lost in the hustle…
    those spontaneous moments
    without children

Smarty-Pants

learning early
instructions are suggestive
when you know it all

my daughter told her mother that she didn't want
baby coloring books anymore so her mother tore
a page out of an adult coloring book for her   it
was the new fad at the time   a book full of wild
designs with hundreds of lines that confine color
& create intricacies   informatively i took an
orange pencil & filled in a tiny sliver of a
butterfly wing telling her to keep it within the
lines   she tugged the pencil from my fingertips
& told me   i know what i'm doing   so i left
her alone with her page of adult relaxation &
went to finish washing the breakfast dishes   a
few minutes later she entered the room proudly
displaying her work   it was more chaotic than
calm   it was a color bomb explosion that had
reached far beyond the confining lines   i said
whoa   what in the world…   she smiled
& said see   i told you so…

memory lane—
all the art stuck to
refrigerators

Cowboy Dream

single malt—
the slow burn
of reality

happy hour   he talked about a dream he'd had
said he thought the strangest thing about it was
that one moment he looked like travolta from
urban cowboy   & the next moment he was
gyllenhaal from brokeback   never haggard
like eastwood   never wayne   never heston
he said he was very curious about the meaning
of it all   why he'd dreamed himself as a couple
of cowboys from love movies & not movies of
gunshots & grit where everyone in town held
their breath & depended on
his rugged badassness
to save the day

The Last Day of August

some fragmented   some complex   some vivid
& some just downright dippy   nobody wins
playing ping pong blindfolded with rubber
mallets & marbles   a waste of time   slowly
strolling through a vineyard at harvest season
the smell & taste of the grapes   sticky juices
how delightful   shoving carrots through
peepholes in backyard fences   dodging
raindrops before 9 a.m. in a london flower
market with a brick wall of a pro wrestler that i
once met in a breckenrigde high school gym
both of us dressed to the nines looking for his
mother   of course there were many untrusting
looks cast our way   yet it didn't stop us   we
searched high & low beyond the market looking
for this lady   but no luck finding her   what a
shame   around one corner was a door with a
sign that read   waiting inside is the love of
your life   he never opened it
neither did i

> like soured wine
> spoiling a good occasion…
> morning alarm clock

6:19 a.m.

a dusk-to-dawn light flickers on the north side
of a church   to the east is a pale peach glow
the sunrise flirts like an ex-lover showing just
enough bare skin to help you remember all those
days of going down south   i turn my head to
the west   it's looking more & more like
another beautiful day to trail
temptations

       dogs chasing cars…
       do they really know
       just what to do
       if they were
       to actually
       catch
       them

September 23, 2025

tiptoeing somewhere around a battlefield
i've never fully known if the moon & i have
ever progressed to the point of loving each other
hanging out there in the distance is a knife
singing   one cup of sugar   one cup of hot
water   combine   mix & stir   three cups of
cool water   combine   mix & stir   mix & stir
it's not much of a song but it's sweet   yesterday
in the front yard we filled the feeders for the
final time this year   sadly   again   all of the
hummingbirds will be leaving soon
without me

      seven months without
      small pieces of happiness…
      the state of affairs

The State of Affairs

in this small carroll town   on an up down
crouched street   in a wood-boxed backyard
you'll find four pumpkins my children spent
hours stabbing & styling up for fun   they
once sat side-by-side on the front porch for
weeks with a burning feeling inside of them
but now that the ghosts have been traded for the
gobbles   the welcoming crew have been cast
out into a pile of warm compost   they are all
slowly becoming disgusting   their slanted
eyes eroding   their demon brows browning
their frightful mouths mushing   love left long
ago   & that rise & fall fluttering feeling is just
the pitchfork turning the pile   soon
the hackberry leaves will fall
& cover it all

    long life
    desires…
    breaking down reality
    we are
    all
    just
    pumpkins

Matthew Freeman

Matthew Freeman's new book, *Dopamine and the Devil* (Coffeetown Press) documents his struggle with schizophrenia and puts it into the context of various discourses. He holds an MFA from the University of Missouri-St Louis.

When You've Outlived the Miracle

You'd like to know
why I'm not a Beatle.
Well, mom, thanks for asking.
The Beatles didn't have to deal
with chronic schizophrenia.
And they didn't live
in a region where every creative impulse
that has nothing to do with money
is resented and quashed.

So as I walked to Schnucks today
with my diabetic foot
and my diabetic leg
I ran my hand
along the metal fence
and when I came to the hollow posts
I made a very loud ding,
each ding louder than the last,
until it seemed as if
the whole world could hear it.

Call a Ride

I'm so sorry but I really, really
don't want to do anything.
I especially don't want to dance in a
crowd. I don't know
why this is. I started
feeling this way
several years ago. I noticed also
that I don't like it
when people wear trendy clothes
or talk about trendy music or actors.

I'm grateful but believe me when I say
that the world is all fucked up.
I never ever get a good feeling about it
anymore. And when I think about my
beautiful dentures I think maybe
everybody should have dentures.
It just seems a whole lot easier
than having to brush your teeth all the time.
I have these really cool shoes
but it hurts when I walk.
There's got to be a shuttle or something
for people like me.

Patina

I saw a priest
in a long black robe
walk into Papa John's
on a terribly sunny day
as I was waiting for a bus
that would never come.

I think maybe trauma's like
tinnitus. After a while
it's just sort of there.

New Ways of Reading

Oh, I became
the sensitive poet.
It's all God's fault.
Because I'd been
a ghastly obnoxious drunk,
spitting out rhymes,
saying such regrettable
stuff. I hate that guy.
But I'm learning
to give him a break.
Because he paid in
to a trauma
that was so much worse than
the one
he was already born with.
It's like you dream
of being a secret agent
and then years later
you wake up to that call:
Meet us
at the federal building.
Come alone. Make sure
you're not followed.

Wanting

I was coming up
on the elevator
thinking of poor Livingston
and all of his prescient mind games
and for a moment
I wished he were here to talk.
What a conversation we would have,
especially now that I'm immune
to all mind games.
I don't have to get high
and go through an awful trip
because I'm already there anyway.
I just need the correct chemicals.

So to conclude and finish
all disputes:
Lesbia told me once, It's poetry.
You can do whatever you want.
So I shall stay gratefully clear.

From My Confinement

I'd like to insert myself
into one of these novels
where the sultry characters
pretend they don't feel anything
and rip on popular culture
and have lots of money
but are also disdainful about it.

I'd like to blow up a novel as such
with eagerness and cheerfulness.
I might be old and paranoid
and completely alone
but I think
I still believe in love. And
I believe in the ultimate presence
of simple sentences
that have no suggestion or pretense.

Romantic

There's a great big emptiness
inside of me.
No, that doesn't sound right.
Nothing has any meaning, it's all coincidence.
That doesn't really make sense either.
I feel like
the ultimate transcendent gesture
is my love for people
I haven't seen in thirty-four years.
It isn't pathetic or miserable.
I've got a million friends
and a mushroom for a brain.

But because I believe
that in some way
words are attached to things
I've taken a heavy beating.
I'm an outlaw, outcast, pariah.

About twenty seconds after
meeting my new advisor at NYU
he said that I was crazy. I quoted
some Rimbaud in terrible French
and he was like,
"Is that supposed to be Rimbaud? You know,
I did my master's thesis on him."

The good news
is if they were all here
to accept my apology
maybe they would recognize
that I was dealing with some tough stuff.
And maybe the reason
that that'll never happen
is that secretly underneath it all
is still the impulse
to tear everything down.

Feverish Pipe Dream

I'm starting to understand
the source
of my suffering.
I think it has to be
the soul.
And these meds are like
putting a band-aid where
an arm's been cut off
by a brutal inquisitor
who didn't like your take
on transubstantiation.
And yes, it's like
saying something over and over
in a slightly different way.
That's just my trip, I guess.

The great beauty would be
getting a piece
about psychosis
into a fabulous journal.

Reminder

I wish I could put language
onto everything
which refuses to be
expressed. The only way
I can explain my dreams
is to say
that concepts and objects
get confused, that words and things
are conflated. Sometimes
a falling leaf might be a great truth
or a sigh. I wish
I could explain the fleeting ecstasy
you get
when you do a whippet.
I'm so belated now.

I suppose I'll never get free
from the constant figuration
of meds, nicotine, Diet Dr Pepper, and
this awful thing they call the world.
I've got real physical problems
but I'm not really worried about that.
Go figure. Get yourself together.
Didn't you at one time actually
play sports?

My Meaning

Have I ever told you
how when I was a little kid
I was really into Rambo and Red Dawn
and really wanted to get it on
with the Soviets?
Oh, what was wrong with me!
It must've been my dad and Vietnam,
Ollie North and old copies
of the National Review.
Thanks to the God
Who blew open my brain when I was a teen.
I would've become a real asshole.

I swear I've never been conscious
of one single thing
my entire life. I don't know what I want
and I don't know why I want it.
I've operated on intuition alone.
Every decision has been aesthetic.
I still dream of running away!

For the longest time
I've been living in this dream world
where nothing
is quite real
and ordinary objects sometimes seem weird.
It comes across—still—as bullshit.

The reason no one would dance with me
during that particular section of gym
was that they somehow knew
that I would grow up to be this way,
utterly divorced from Kapital
and displaced into pure hermeneutics.

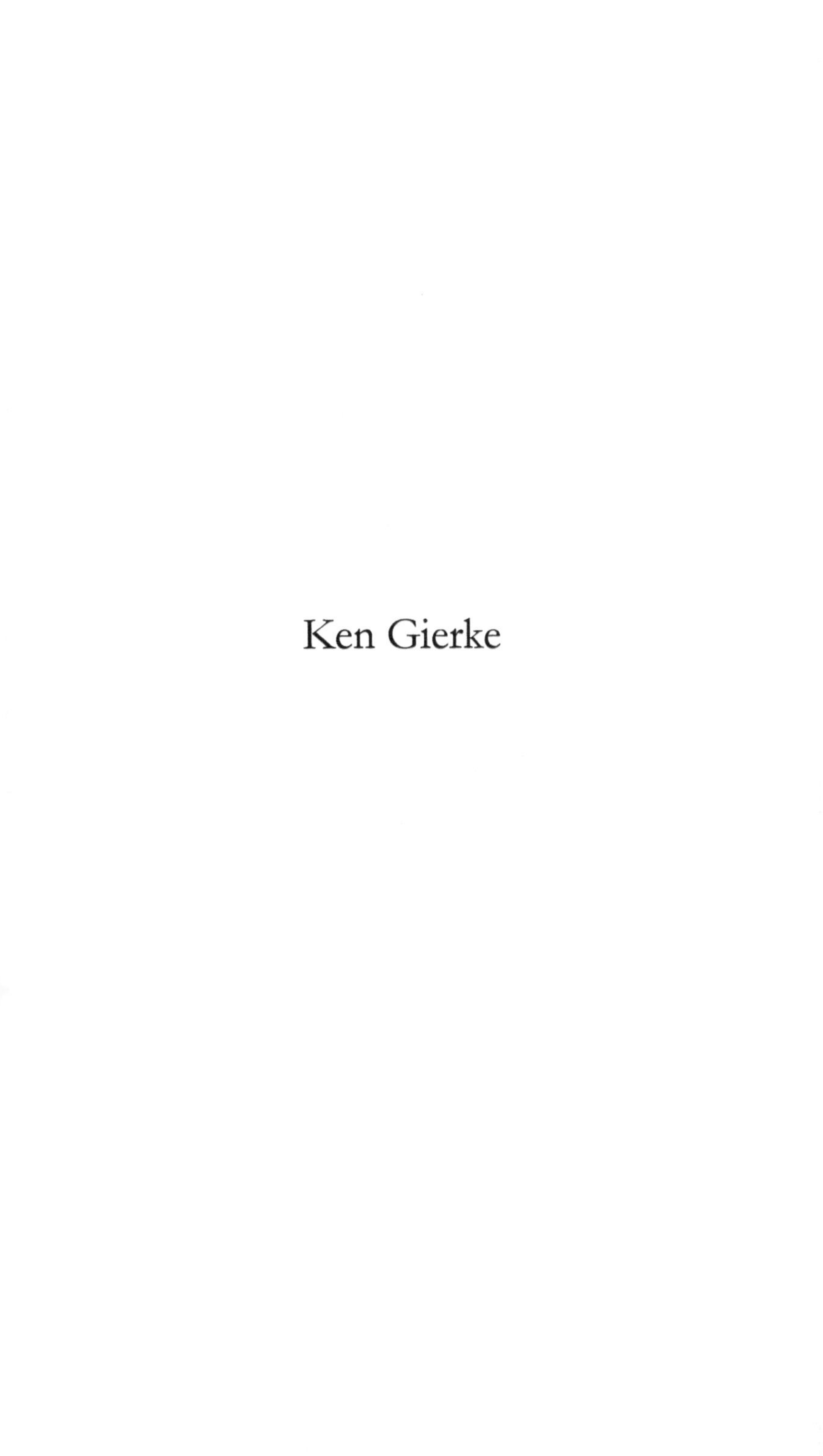

Ken Gierke

Transplanted from Western New York, **Ken Gierke** has lived in Missouri since 2012. Twice nominated for a Pushcart Prize, his writing has appeared as two micro-chapbooks from Origami Poems Project and in numerous anthologies, including *River Dog Zine* and the *Gasconade Review*. His poetry collections, *Glass Awash* in 2022, *Heron Spirit* in 2024, and *Random Riffs* in 2025, were published by Spartan Press. His website: https://rivrvlogr.com/

One Way or Another

Did you know?
Did you fear?
Did you brush it all aside?

We thought we knew.
But did we understand how short
your time with us would be?

Over the years, they tried to tell you,
but what do doctors know?
Life is for living. For you, to the fullest.

When blood sugar can only be tested
by the doctor, avoid sweets the week before.
You were only fooling yourself.

You knew better in your later years,
but it caught up to you. It was too late.
For all of us, it was too early.

My early years, it turns out,
were your middle years.
Before my middle years, you were gone.

One Last Door

Doctors distant as the city
does not mean illness will not visit
or ignore any door left open
by a lifetime taken for granted.

Medicine is stopgap,
unable to remedy old habits
paused for doctor visits,
resumed until the next appointment.

The future waits,
until it runs its course,
takes its final toll
once the last door is closed.

Don't Lose Heart

To the heart of the matter
Have a heart
Know this by heart
Take heart
To your heart's content
Wear your heart on your sleeve
Whole-heartedly
Straight from the heart
Take it to heart
Heart is normal sized
Follow your heart
Know this with all your heart
Find it in your heart
To your heart's content
Your heart is in the right place
Keep it close to your heart
Anxiety gnaws at the heart
You may have a change of heart
The heart size is enlarged
Don't lose heart
You still have a heart

Sikeston to Memphis

Missouri into Arkansas.
Mississippi ten miles,
no, a quarter-mile,
no, five miles to the left,
west, running south,
muddy and high,
even if today's light rain
doesn't tell the story
of yesterday's deluge.
Every other farm field
underwater. Telephone poles
at sea, their nearest shoreline
the interstate. Bridge pothole
five inches deep
wearing water as camo
rattles teeth at 70 mph, swallows
tire, spits it right back out,
just in time to look down
at stream passing two feet
below the bridge. Clever marketing,
Five Star Truck Wash
billboard in flooded field.
Leave the farms behind
to cross the muddy river
into Memphis, a dry land
respite that doesn't tell the story
of the new wetlands that surround it.

Freddie Freeloader

Slow and lazy, Miles' horn
opens the tune, subtle
bass, piano, and percussion
nudging it along as I climb
into the truck, passenger side,
a rare occasion. Anesthesia
doing its best to hang on, though
wearing off as we drive away
from the surgery center,
wants to hold onto that horn
as long as possible.

Piano takes over, a conversation
about my procedure, details
rattled off as if I remember
any of it, but a percussive beat,
fingers snapping me out of it,
reminds me I'm just waking up.

The horn seems to wake up
as we head for a late lunch.
Twenty hours after my last meal,
I feel the hunger gnawing at me,
Coltrane and Adderly on sax
adding impetus. Piano, bass
and percussion come out front
to lead into the horn, smooth,

but punctuated by sax
as Freddie Freeloader exits and
I leave the truck for some chow.

Have a Safe Flight

Broadway, the brewpub
where the stout goes down
smooth, like the flight,
make that flights,
in the stories told
by the man three seats over,
his son with his turboprop
going here, there,
giving an old man
the vicarious pleasure
of expendable wealth
as he drinks the same beer
as me and buys the cheapest
item on the lunch menu,
satisfied to have that
in his life.

Blue-Collar Winter

Tan Carhart coveralls
blue jeans and red
or blue plaid shirts
for a blue-collar worker.

Short winter days,
long nights of work
on frigid loading docks.
Trailers shuttled around the yard,
driving through snow blowing
white in the inky darkness,
face ruddy from the blowing wind.

Only relief from the cold
during brief breaks,
inside, hands warmed against
the beige porcelain of a coffee mug,
its rich black brew savored.

Coveralls shed at end-of-shift
to don a blue puffer jacket
and drive through that same snowfall,
its flakes a pattern of white
dancing in my headlights,
this drive ending with
the warmth of home
at the end of a blue-collar day.

Treading Water

Did we really stand by burning barrels,
our hands held out from the cold
while placards on sticks leaning
against the barrels dried as the snow
on them melted away, the night
no shorter, only colder than the long
day of walking back and forth
with a desire to keep a living wage
without giving up job security?

I know we were united in our cause,
but that didn't guarantee an outcome
that would make everyone happy.

The fires would go out. The barrels
would be pushed aside to rust outside
the gates that welcomed us back as if
we were never gone, just happy to get
a check that didn't make up for lost wages.

For the Many

One class, one caste to include everybody.
None are immune here.
This disease that plagues us today is
intent on adding to the infirm.

One class, one caste to include everybody.
None are immune here.
Your failure to recognize this is
sure to take a toll on the infirm.

You say you have survived, but oh,
some are not so quick to mend.
You may scoff at what I say, ridicule me,
but some will never mend.
It could have been you. It may be me.
This does not make you better, a lord.

I read the signs, the news today,
and understand I am one of many, that I
am exposed when you say
you have no need to fear, to
take caution, that you are not one of them.

Despite what you say,
you, too, are of the many. Others act to
protect their fellows, protect them

with no thought to say
they cannot be troubled, to
act as though they care not for them.

For they do, with no thought to lord
it over the many. Their desire to look
out for their fellow man, you and I,
is a sign that you are, that I am,
valued, and that is beautiful.

When the common and the beautiful
are seen as equal and viewed with
compassion, that is when my
true respect for others takes wing.

Our strength rises when that
understanding of equality is
wedded with a desire to spare the wounded.

There should be no "my,"
only "our." When we see eye to eye,
when we come to realize that
the key to our survival is
best served when the many are bonded,
we will prevail. That, or

suffer the loss of my
sister or your mother, a deaf ear
turned to the grief that will not
serve sentiments funded

towards the consideration of others, or
even ourselves. Your regard for my
well-being should come unbidden. We walk
the same path. A beginning. An end. All
else may differ, but all else is a-wobble.

All is insanity, to think that I'm
insignificant to you, little enough
to trouble your mind, to
mask your pretension of superiority. Be
more than that. Be beautiful.

Let the world see that in you.
Join those who believe that others are
no less than beautiful.
Be one who thinks of others, too.

Botsford Hollow

Trudging down country roads,
legs lifted with each step
in the snow, the glazed tracks
left by passing pickups
too slick for walking.

The crisp snap of cold air
against the backs of
our throats with each
drawn breath as painful
as it was exhilarating.

Not so much, winter's bite
on our cheeks as we raced
across snow-covered fields,
down those same country roads,
on Arctic Cats faster than
any pickup with sand bags
in the bed begging for traction.

The warmth of your stove,
wood burning and glowing
through slits in the door,
on fingers and toes that burned
from the cold of a winter day
but yearned for another day
just like this.

Anna Lum

Anna Lum teaches Tai Chi (since 1973). She evolved from computer programming to poetry/design. *The Urge to Play God*, published by MoonShadow Press led to performing her poetry nationally and internationally. St. Louis' first Poet Laureate Michael Castro's new anthology *Crossing the Divide* includes her poem "Sitting Down for Yourself"Volunteering excessively on numerous arts boards she was named St. Louis Woman of Achievement in cultural awareness in 2002.

Drop a Quark

Drop a quark
in any thought pond in space
Watch the universe quiver.

Boxes

The next box
of memories
moving to the basement
will be the proverbial straw
In one flash
the floor, the walls cry out
no more, no more
crumble and flee
to the earth's core
past water lines, gas lines
the sewers yearning
to be free
of the weight
of the years
of the things
that keep
piling up.

Eating Chinese

There are no boundaries
to eating Chinese.
Once, a nine-course feast
was the benchmark
Now, they catapult to thirty
The Chongqing hot pot
cannot be...forgive me...forgot
Take a ten-foot round table
add an eight-foot lazy suzan
laden with duck tongues,
cow's stomach, intestines
pig gonads, kidneys, tripe
fish bladder, all raw
The waiters do not stop,
more exotica piling up,
balanced on each other
Each diner has a pot
fired from below and within
Stock exponentially hot
we can cook and eat at our
pleasure. No end to the toasts
with twenty at the table
Gan bei, bottoms up
Glasses for beer, like juice
are small, but bottomless.
Our hosts' faces are turning
traditional Chinese red

while we westerners
keep our cool rising
on this cultural crossing
that keeps returning.

Strip of Mobius

Salome and Gypsy Rose take note
tonight, we present
the strip of Mobius
a never-ending delight
where every end is a new beginning

I turn on the strip
where the more I remove
the more there remains
I climb up Escher's stairs
and meet myself skipping down
to find the missing chink
in the tai chi player
star-struck by Gypsy Rose
schooled by Salome
What color is a chameleon
posing before a mirror?
this is the end

The Edge

I dance the line
between sun and shade
mindless
of the danger
at the edge
where sun falls
93 million miles
and escapes
the tall pines
caught now
by a blade of grass
Too small for my body
Still, I dance.

Point of Acupressure

for Rachel

Armed with Gach's
Acupressure's Potent Points
I flew back to Boulder
The doctor had discovered
one fetus was not growing as well
inside my oldest daughter Rachel
thirty-four weeks pregnant with twins.

All hooked up and wired
for the nurses to monitor
her contractions
She was being
induced, but
not much was happening
when I entered her hospital room.

Not formally trained in acupressure
decades of playing Tai Chi
filled my body/mind with free flowing Qi
I found those points on Rachel's hands and feet
to assist childbirth and
surreptitiously pushed
whenever the western doctor was gone.

Late afternoon, the doctor examines
Rachel and finds her dilating well.
He's seen the graph of greater contractions
when Rachel and I are alone.

To me he says
Mom, keep doing whatever you're doing
And leaves the room.

Elated am I to have paper proof
of physical affects of Qi energy
By eight thirty that night
my fourth and fifth grandkids
were naturally born
and grew in the NICU
till they were full term.

The Talk of the Delta

From the height of Victoria Falls
far better named mosi-oa-tunya
the smoke that thunders
on the bridge that crosses the Zambezi
she stands halfway to her 69th birthday
Barely over the quota at 92 lbs
torso strapped, lower legs towel wrapped
together and tied to the bungi cord
she is blind without her glasses
Fellow safari travelers
and other stranger strangers declare
Chinese women are strong
cheer and watch in fear
Her knees are trembling
as the countdown starts
Five...four...three...two
She pushes off the edge
arms spread
in a perfect swan dive
Her maroon polo caught
forever on Debbie's video
She is free
from her father's admonitions
BE CAREFUL...be careful
from each step taken
with thoughtful care
from fear of caterpillars down her shirt

from fear of skiing a Wisconsin slope
From the outside you'd never guess
what guts dwell in there.
No wonder my big sister, Joyce
is the talk of the Okavanga Delta.

Taking That Step

When a father escapes
that straitjacket
rolled in the mind
of a daughter
A human is born

He left school at eighteen
for work to support the family
Careful details his mind
His hands
fit post office needs
leads to Ho Ying-Chin
future general of
Kuomintang
Secretary of Defense
My father, the general's aide
his right hand man
wrote his speeches in
unparalleled calligraphy
traveled at his side
in China and USA
to form the United Nations

I marvel at my father's decision
when the UN delegation
returned to Taiwan
He chose to stay in USA

with his four children
his second wife, no language
no money, no degrees, no job

More opportunity for us
his children here in America

He started a salesman
Chinese art products
with me just eight at his side
Door to door in New Rochelle
I loved being with him alone.
Piece work paid more
Pennies per hole he drilled
gemstones for high school rings
while he babysat my stepsister.
Columbia University awarded him
Master's Degree in Education
No college degree, no high school diploma
he will build the first high school
in his native Guizhou
Communists changed his future
Instead he built the official
Plexiglas model the 1964
World's Fair in New York
numerous pre-production
models for Kodak.
He sang Chinese opera in Onondaga cave.

Sitting Down for Yourself

At the corner of Utah and Lemp
in nearly historic St. Louis
sits an underground home to noise
concerts, some on two days notice
Improvising musicians, performance artists
en route from here to there
test the local water
Last night one Emil from Lowell
Massachusetts took a test
You can decide if he passed or failed.

Rich and I also on a concert circuit
this time on the listening end
hit this place at 10:30 pm
Emil's raucous voice greets us
Admission $7.00, that includes
a $2 late fee. We laugh and pay.

The audience is standing
at the far end of the room
fifty years younger bobbing to the
deafening turntable and Emil's
parody of Mr. Rogers,
crooked, boorish, working
hard at anti-establishment.
Momentarily done but for the sweating
Emil notices us
sitting not standing.

That's taboo for Emil.
Planting himself in front of us
he motions with his thumb
Stand Up!
Our thumbs turn
Stand down.
Stand UP!
Stand down.

This confrontation goes on and on
Stand up! He stamps his feet
a spoiled child not getting his way
Rich replies with a Soweto beat
Emil stomps now a martial tone
and conducts the crowd to shout
STAND UP! Again and again
STAND UP!

Would we be swayed by peer pressure?
Of course not, and we sit, still, not moving.
Tearing his hair Emil works the crowd into a mob
Are you going to stand for this?
ARE YOU GOING TO STAND FOR THIS?!!
The mob rushes across the room like hooligans
lifts up the couch and dumps us on the ground.

I love siting on the floor
That doesn't bother me
but the frenzy of the mob so easily led
leads my mind to Hitler and Clockwork Orange.

This physical act calms Emil and the crowd
He concludes and crows
when you're so old and decrepit
you can't stand up
To which I reply in my best Tai Chi voice
At the rate you're going, Emil,
you'll never survive to our age.

Forty-Three Days To Go

*My mother died when I was four, leaving me no memories. When I turned
38, my father gave me my first photo of her taken at the same age, 43
days before her death.*

Not prone to regretting
I never dreamed the day away Not prone to
   dreaming
I never regretted moonlight bathing my cheeks
streaming my hair with stars I never cried into the
night Mama, wherever you are Keep watch, keep
   watch.
Yet today we meet in two dimensions You do not
exceed my expectations Your take my hand We slip
through wax The cardboard years dissolve
You move easily I have your ease You do not speak
I watch your feet
We walk through thick leaves Thick air leaves my
   hair steaming
Or was it a sudden downpour But your feet are not
   damp
I would have seen
your cotton black shoes drink.
Not content to loll in bed Yangtze River rose instead
covering Chongqing with thick air September
we are there and Daddy adds the third dimension

You two sit touching the wooden bench on which I
   lean
nestled between his right arm draped across your

shoulder Your hand still holds mine resting in your lap
    softly
My left hand clutches Daddy's knee The wrinkles are
still there. I can see his hand on mine, his knees lined
straight over his feet, his body lean
taut, caught between family and the war.
Your face distraught behind distorting glasses.
You must know
Forty three days to go
I keep watching
for a light in your eyes
The only moon is your face No stars in your hair
Where, where, where
am I in you?
I am as you were
in the fourth dimension Shall I leave my daughters no
    regretting
and all the stars you left me
That they can dream the day And watch me
As I do you today.

Chris Nico

Chris Nico is a poet from Pacific, Missouri, where art-making and caregiving share the same messy, beautiful space. They raise four children with the support of their community and partner, Ben. Two kids split time between Mexico and the U.S. following the deportation of their father. Chris shares a deeply intertwined life with Julianne King, their best friend of 26 years. Together they have built a deliberate family. Surrounded by chickens, guinea pigs, and a cat, Chris writes poetry that moves through religion, love, heartbreak, and rage. Intimate work that holds tenderness in one hand and fire in the other.

The grieving process was not long
When compared to the amount of time you stole
My best years
Wasted
My free years
Squandered
For purity I will never attain
For reward I will never taste
Because they don't exist
There's always been one set of footprints
& they've always been mine

I keep cutting out
a piece of my heart
every time you even hint at being hungry
& for some reason
It never occurred
to either of us
that you could just make your own
god damn sandwich

I promised to bring down the wall
But I know I am a lot
It will be brick by brick
Stones around your feet
One at a time
I hope you don't drown

If the love isn't
Stop-this-car-and-run-across-four-lanes-of-
    interstate-
to-pick-wildflowers-for-you-because-that-shade-
periwinkle-doesn't-exist-anywhere-else
Then I don't want it

For there to be
those of peace,
There must be
Those of war

I do not desire to be soft
Instead, hardened
I do not desire to be kind
Instead, just

I will protect
I will meet the world
Where it has met me

I hope I become archaic
Outdated
But until then
I will sharpen my knife

You have a distance to you

& I've killed myself in that lonely expanse before
Sank down in the quicksand of your heart
Bloodied my hands on every part of you
Tried to feel enough
For both of us

& if you ever loved me
You wouldn't invite me back in again

We are loosely stitched together
With electricity

Swaying sparks
Suspended
Between us

A live wire
The fates keep pulling

Us closer and closer
Together

Around the time I make the coffee
Is the time I realize
You're not here

Sometimes it's when
I switch the kettle on
Sometimes I catch myself
Reaching for you mug

John Green made me believe
The thing you'd miss the most
About someone
Is the way they smell

But I'd give anything
To put anything
In your hand

I would never begrudge
Whatever light
You find in the dark

Fuck it
Let it be vape light

As long as it
Get you out
To stand in the sun
With me

The hallway always smells
like a really good tea
after your bath
& I know this sounds like
a poem about how I want
to drink your bathwater
But it's just about how
you always make it better
than you found it

Sharon SingingMoon

Sharon SingingMoon is a poet, an award-winning visual artist and host of a monthly reading series, SPOKEN at Café Berlin. Her work appears in several anthologies and has been widely published in the US, the UK and Europe. She is co-editor of *Well Versed* 2024 and 2025 and *Rough-Cut Elegies, An Anthology of Missouri Poets* (Spartan Press). She is the founding editor of the *Watermelon Seeds Anthology Project,* publisher of *Soul of Our Soul – Palestine in Poetry and Prose,* 2025, a collection of poetry and prose to benefit the children of Palestine who have been wounded and traumatized by violence. Sharon's work has been nominated for Best of the Net 2025, 3 times for a Pushcart Prize; and for an Eric Hoffer Book Award. Her collections, *The Weight of One Hummingbird Feather* (Spartan Press), *Random Seed* (Compass Flower Press), and *Soul of Our Soul* (Watermelon Seeds Project) can be found at independent bookshops across the mid-West and on Barnes & Nobel and Amazon. Visit Sharon at www.singingmoonseestheworld.com

At Last

We want to rest, to find a forest, branches spread
a welcome to the peace we long for
amidst the growing human chaos
the politic of war
killing of innocence
rupture in the human soul
a place where tears offer up prayers
a place where heartbeats attune to the rhythm
of earth's wordless song
come, lie with me in this mossy wonderland
let your breath slow, your soul respond to
the music of the flowing stream
all human frailties become mist
rising to dissipate
as mountains laugh at our struggles
granite comforts with whispers of eons
a world alive
before, beyond us
trees reach down to caress
where we recognize at last
we are one
with the beauty of this garden
where our small, senseless triumphs
ring hollow as life around us
vibrates

we do what it takes

to save those we love
shelter our family put
food on the table
but
would you dig through
the rubble of your bombed-out
house barehanded, bleeding
praying they are alive
to find the bodies of your children
carry the bones of your new born
in a plastic bag because that's all
you have left
would you run after a truck
knowing you may be shot
just for a bag of flour would
you kneel in the dust
to scrape up bits of food
after those with guns
tore through your home
stealing, breaking, destroying
would you walk into the tide
watching where they drop
for a box of MRE's
soaked in sea water would
you humiliate yourself for
a bottle of water
knowing your child
is being
starved?

**Walking with Monks & Rebels
In Total Resistance**

We were to change the world
make an effort anyway
marching for/to justice
that fantasy of humanity
unrecognized in a life of terror & trauma
we sat in lodges, sweat streaming, smoke carrying hope
mornings we ate cold oatmeal
between chants, knees in the frosty grass
prayer drums held high
twenty miles a day & setting up a camp
hot stone soup renewed determination
sleep came fast

We were to change the world
fight for it
put our bodies where we could testify
teach as we passed
leave at least one who promised to carry on
repeat the names & dates of each treaty
compromised forgotten dismissed
each woman sterilized without
her knowing we
committed to the walk
to each other
unity bred of anger & compassion
ceremonies ancient renewed

We were to change the world
make an effort
lifting up in spite of our own failings
protectors in cold tents
staring down the weapons of war
fear of our power on their minds
insults & threats on their lips
future generations our treasures
not beggars but pleading for some ideal
clean water air fresh
care for fellow travelers
respect

My Body Ain't Your Business

see this
yes, I mean this right here
these bones and eyes
this flesh and heart,
hair and uterus, yes I said it
uterus
this beautiful creation
sacred space
of blood and salt and muscle
is mine
bequeathed to me alone by
that Great Mystery
the only thing I will ever truly have in this lifetime
is this body
and it ain't your business
this body is mine
to navigate through this beautiful world
to experience, feel
and choose, yes, I said choose
choose where it takes me
how and what I choose to do
with my body
ain't none of your business
as women we've been chattel
status symbols, subjugated play things
money-makers, breeders
we've been denied, demeaned, even damned

but we are fighters, thinkers, poets, lovers
scientists, scholars, owners of our own bodies
we are choice-makers
who, what, how and when
these are choices
that we each have a right to make
'cause my body ain't your business

Latinos

"Let me wash the dirt of misery off your soul"

Latinos

And does this world truly need another poet?
especially one so dark in body & sadness
banging his heart against the rocks of humanity's sins
screaming out our collective endurance for pain
so all will hear

Another rubber raft packed with Africans hopeful
floating from Libya
more trouble coming to the northern shore
should we even find the time between the five & dime
& arrogant disregard
to read his tears merging into the salty
Mediterranean

When probable death becomes the better option
how much is lost what beauty is shut out behind
the boundaries of otherness

A testament to torment
swaying in the sea
his final thought another poem he will never write
perhaps that one perfect poem
this world needs to hear to turn us from our folly
could he have been that "Last-minute savior"
come to rescue this world's body

**Abdel Wahab Yousif, known as Latinos, was a Sudanese Poet. He drowned while trying to cross the Mediterranean Sea in a rubber raft packed with African immigrants.*

Diane Keaton Died Today

the lilac bush down by the shed has a second
      blooming –
it's October here & I wonder
where the groundhogs that lived under Juanita's
sunporch have gone – last week her house was
      demolished
now heavy machinery rumbles all day long
rubble loaded into dumpsters is hauled away –
more than twenty truckloads

I think about the miles & miles of rubble that once
was Gaza – how many loads of homes &
bones will be needed to haul it all – where will it go

they said Diane Keaton died today – she
was seventy-nine – older than the country
that's still bombing & killing –
ignoring the latest ceasefire
booby-trapping toys & food
to explode when touched by hungry children

Diane Keaton died today
the groundhogs found a new den &
Israel assassinated another journalist -
Saleh Al Jaafarawi – number 271 -
he was twenty-eight

Anthropocentric Amnesia

forgotten is the salty sea bleeding through our veins
sounds that call us back
longing for that sand
moonlight dancing on water
seeking home
we wander
as our sisters swim serenely -
living by their own code
brothers not bound by hubris
ask nothing of humanity
forgotten is the sacred soil from which we arose
naked - then
removed ourselves
separated – declared
dominion
over all seen
secretly knowing
we are nothing but clay
& possibilities
never to be achieved
forgotten is the connection to all
life - we take
mistake our temporary ability
arbitrary
capricious
self-proclaiming superiority
yet continually destroying
forgotten is the way back
resting on the tips of our hearts

A Visa Granting the Resurrection of Her Heart

Gradually grief like an old Blues song
twanging out the broken bits
unashamed, finally
sends ribbons of red across the swimming sky
her apprehension a product of personal
growth - so shakily she recalls the love
that seemed so fertile – the sour taste of it
dissipates
floats away with the scent of honeysuckle
on a damp May morning --
so much a recovery
a resurrection of her lobed heart, lungs
that struggle with the need for air -
breath/breathe/breathe --
and now
committed to the ride toward tomorrow
she smiles and wonders
"Will there be peanuts on this flight of fancy?"

Pays better than screwing bowling trophies together

In a third-rate bar
10 pm to closing
we dance in a bay window
on a tiny stage
hanging upside down
on a pole
wearing little
we have our fans
old men who give
us nickel bags
for tips
everyone knows the drinks
they buy us are
watered down
but the weed
we roll in toilet paper
smoke in the bathroom
we do what we can
work with what we've got
rent to pay
a broke-down ride
an abusive ex
who won't go quietly
we are dancers
we are women
we are mothers
with kids to feed

An Accumulation of Loss & Love

She's been carrying her belongings out for weeks now
removing bits of the past – flotsam & jetsam
memories swirling on a rough sea
how her husband gone for years, died in their bed
her son grown & married with his own kids & home
she sorted through each room
packed the scraps of living into cars & hired vans
took her time holding some items close
a final moment before letting go
what matters - small boxes of photos
documents that legitimize her being
prove she & her life are of consequence
were hauled to a rental space
leaving some for the demo team & dumpsters
she ignored the dark & damp of the basement
not wishing to resuscitate things
abandoned, forgotten
toys no longer relevant to her or her son
treasures the grandkids would not treasure
some she took away to her new apartment -
furniture, kitchen necessities, clothing
plans for her new life - hopes
agreements, contracts with experts signed
modern lifelines – water, electricity – disconnected
the day arrived
within two hours her home of thirty-five years
reduced to a pile of twisted rubble
filled dumpsters as if it had never been
a place filled with love

Clarence Wolfshohl

Clarence Wolfshohl, professor emeritus at William Woods University, has been active in the small press as writer and publisher for over fifty years, publishing poetry and non-fiction in many journals, both print and online, including *North Dakota Quarterly, Concho River Review, San Pedro River Review, Agave, Green Hills Literary Lantern, Cape Rock, New Letters, Southwestern American Review, Gasconade Review, Home Planet News,* and *The Mailer Review.* Among his recent publications are the e-chapbook *Scattering Ashes* (Virtual Artists Collective, 2016), the chapbooks *Holy Toledo* (El Grito del Lobo Press, 2017), *Queries and Wonderments* (El Grito del Lobo Press, 2017), *Armadillos & Groundhogs* (2019), *Scattering Ashes* (El Grito del Lobo, 2025), and his collection *Play-Like* (Alien Buddha Press, 2025). He has been nominated for a Pushcart Prize twice. Wolfshohl lives in the suburbs of Toledo, Missouri, with his two cats.

The Fruit of Innocence

Thomas Hart Benton's Persephone

She's older than I'd think,
all those accounts of her and the maidens
gathering flowers in spring meadows.
And Hades, too, more a middle-aged man
than a primal force, a chthonic urgency.

He reminds me of my neighbor
who raises a few head of cattle
and acres of feed corn. The field
of sheaves beckons in the distance,
but he is in no hurry to gather them.

He gazes on Persephone,
his long laboring fingers inches
from her hip. Her hip is not round
in virginal succulence, more angular
to reflect Hades's creviced face.

And her face, as she reclines
in pin-up calendar pose, is a knowing face.
The curve of light of nose and brow
hints of eyes closed by choice not chance
as if she anticipates his first touch.

Before Hades's deed the world
was in perpetual spring, all flowers,

all innocence. Her mother's tears
created the seasons, so the story goes.
But what of fruit, of gathered sheaves?
The knowing face?

Smoke on the Horizon

The Paintings of Thomas Hart Benton

It may be that wide band of sinuous black
that bellows energy above streets and shacks
of Boomtown, anticlined to telegraph poles,
derricks, drilling towers; or it may roll
a thin racing line from a locomotive stack
or steamboat at Huck and Jim's backs.

It may be roiling clouds from the earth formed
in the twisting winds before prairie hailstorm,
or the earth ablaze from bombs and guns
in Year of Peril or Atlanta burning in Hollywood sun,
or fire itself from the mouth of a drowning man
on a Starry Night torpedoed far from land.

Smoke on the horizons of Benton's art
mirrors the shapes of the human heart.

Eye Hook

The cypress has grown
through the eye
to absorb it in years
of annual rings,
to encase that pupil
in its half circle
wink now.

The chrome socket
glints back
in midnight
trotline light,
and a pair
of silver green dots
stare back
in the flash,
blink and slide
behind brush.

Water, drop
by drop from raised
line, like tears
of a sobbing child.

On a Cold December Day

Three deer—two does
and a yearling—nuzzle seeds
dropped from the bird feeder.

They are glad the flickers
and jays are so unmannerly
and messy. A dove

waddles at the yearling's
hooves, pecks at seeds,
puffs its feathers against the chill.

One squirrel claws at suet
hanging from a cedar limb.
another acrobats around

the sunflower seed cage.
All alert to a dry crack
or rustle of leaf litter.

Little Peggy March at the Y

The noise comes from halfway around the track.
Like a cat's mew at night, a cry of injury, anguish, joy?
Only three of us walk the track, another old guy
who well could be whimpering. Or is that me?

But as I gain on the third walker—a woman
with ear buds streaming her music in silence—
I hear her translating that silent song
in a barely whispered voice until the rising chorus

in full vibrato, which I can't remember
from Little Peggy March's 1963 "I Will Follow Him"
but is now resounding all over the track at the Y
thanks to this teeny-bopping septuagenarian.

Nectar

fritillaries bounce
      on the air
           around me

      nearly daring
to light and sip

      the sweat off my brow

as I weed
      the garden three feet
           from the milkweed patch

purple blooms   bear up
hundreds of butterflies
      in that ten by ten jungle

         a lone sweat bee
      safaris through
      my arm hair
         to siphon off
the nectar of my sweat

his cousins of several species
share the milkweed pollen
         and nectar
with the butterflies.

Looking at Hammersmith Bridge

From a Spot in Hammersmith Park

[Poet's note: In his old age, not wishing anyone to continue using the Doves Press typeface, William Cobden-Sanderson, co-founder of Doves Press, carried the matrices of the type in his pockets as he took his daily walk and threw them into the Thames as he crossed Hammersmith Bridge. -- learned from Lionel Selwyn, London printer]

In the distance, Hammersmith Bridge,
where the old, mad printer emptied pockets
of doves into the Thames. He walked
each night from this spot
perhaps through those roses
with great yellow heads, perhaps
around those drunks sleeping underneath.

He could not let the letters sleep
to be awakened by warmer hands. So he walked
from here with pockets full, ready to cast
the lead like breadcrumbs to pigeons hungry
for words or, pointedly, to the fish
who took those hooks of serifs and gathered
wing against the fading sun.

Lizard Poem

These things rush from me
today like lizards on a picket
fence or air from a blow-out.
Poems like lizards—
anoles with throats as bright
as fireworks—scooting up
tree trunks in appropriate
green. They are so fast I
wonder if they are really there.
Lizard or flutter of leaves,
I'm not sure.

                    Poems as flat
tires—now we've all had those,
but the meter is dynamic until
the tire shreds and knocks
the mud from the recesses of our
fenders. And that's an admirable
function of poetry: to clean out the
muck that's collected on cross-
country trips.

Gloves of Spanish Leather

one of them left his gloves
fine pair of gloves
'made of Spanish leather' gloves

I don't know if they
really are of Spanish leather
or what is Spanish leather

just leather from Spain?

or from a Spanish type
cow or goat or kangaroo?

or is the leather from a Spaniard?
supple but thin   fits
your hands like
a second skin

Gypsy Davy the gypsy king
had those gloves of Spanish leather

he could have tanned
a Spaniard's hide
perhaps Sancho Panza
or the old Don himself
a much bruised and scarred hide

these gloves the one left

are a fine pair

but just cowhide

or calfskin   probably from Nebraska

Great Serpent Mound

Adams County, Ohio

The observation tower
        is closed for repairs--
                20th-century construction
                already in need
                while below
        down the slope
        slithers centuries
    of successful
shaping. The tail
wraps in a tight
    curlicue. Then
        the serpent creeps
                in sinuous progress
                downhill with a triad
        of slinks until it gradually
        stretches into its open maw
        with the circle of the sun
                perched over the fifty-foot
                    drop to Brushy Creek
                among the woods fringing
            the entire coiling structure.
        Without the tower
        the meanders are
    rises visible but distinct
only as a narrow fellow
in the grass is a minor
disturbance of motion.

Not enough to see
      the rock and soil,
            yellow clay and ash,
                  which are its body,
                  and its body is constantly
                        threatened by the
                        trees so that signs dot
                  the meanders, warning
"Do not stand on the mound."

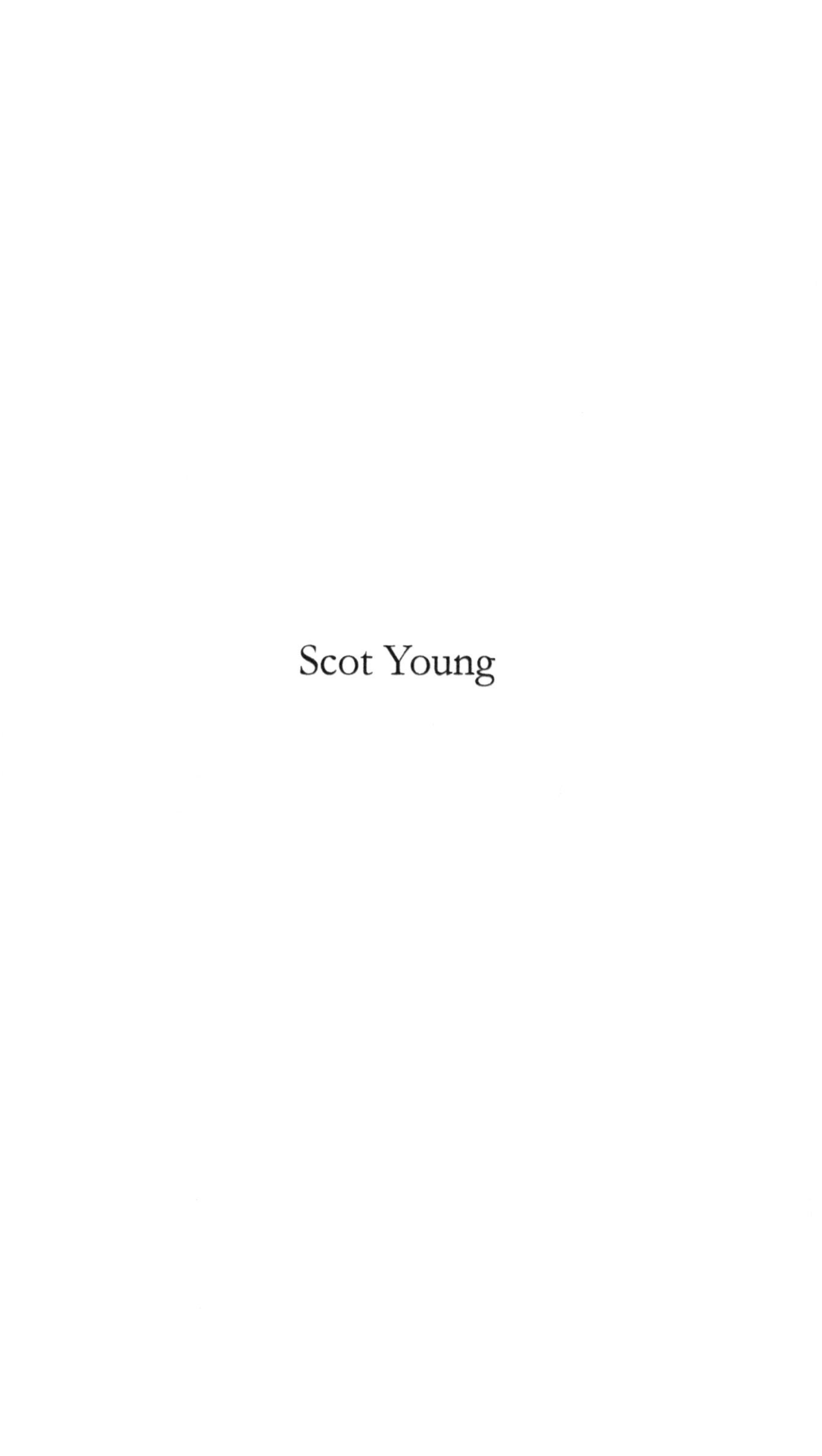

Scot Young

In 1960 **Scot Young** watched Hopalong & Roy
Rogers from a green naguhyde sofa stitched in
cowboys & bucking broncos complete with wagon
wheel arms. On Saturday mornings he cocked his
Red Ryder rifle before ARs and AKs before the
country went to hell in a hate basket when the good
guys always won.

first gig

we were a teenage cover band
played *louie louie*
wipeout & *house of the risin sun*
from the back of a hay wagon
right behind the original
jc penney
hamilton missouri
my mama's town
my family tree
sitting around squinting
into the setting sun

great uncle whit
just starched overalls
pointing one shaky finger
at me singing
said oh hell
them's city boys
turned and
spit brown juice
in an empty cup
ten feet away

boys of summer

in 1965
dad took me to my first
baseball game
kansas city a's
municipal stadium on brooklyn
down by 18th & vine
saw my first black kid up close
parked our impala in his yard
next to the porch
for a buck

his whole family sat spread out
across the porch
the black man
collecting dollar bills
smiled a lot and shook his
head up and down
the boy and i stared
at each other
maybe waiting for the other
to blink

the a's normally lost
and that afternoon
campy campaneris played
every position
as a publicity stunt

and dad made me a magaphone
out of paper beer cups
to cheer the kelley green and gold
after the game i carried
my pennant back to the car
peanuts stuffed in my pockets
nobody was on the porch
& the a's of course lost
that summer i wanted
to be called campy
playing our sandlot ball
on vacant lots
a white cuban growing up in the burbs
in 1965 we all wanted something
we couldn't have

song for maryl

we broke up in 69
my band played
your junior high dance
and i sang you a song
i just wrote
about our teen love
and broken hearts
brought you to tears
which was probably
my intent and
we moved on as kids do
never spoke again
at 23 you wrote
your own song
about broken hearts
with carbon monoxide
in a closed up garage
full tank of gas
slow idle...

i never
wrote another song
for no other reason
than just because.
i don't remember
the lyrics now but
50 years later

i can still
see your eyes
every time
you smiled
i will sing that
song
i know
all the words

ray

got outta prison in 82
pulled up to the job site in a caddy
trunk full of sansabelts
banlons and a dozen leather jackets
big bob said
fuck ray we don't wear that shit
got any flannel shirts & jeans
ray
narrowed his eyes
like eastwood in hang 'em high
remembering the last thing
his daddy said right before
he it the ground

best part of you ran down
your momma's leg

brains and eggs after
the main event

we
left
jerry's
after
the
bar
closed
in
bulldog's
eldorado
headed
to nichol's
lunch
when
murdoch
pulled
a .357
spun
the
cylinder
& shot
a hole
through
the
backseat
floorboard

at 39th
& main
when
my
ears
quit
ringing
we were halfway
through
our brains
and eggs

all around cowboy

after the rodeo
at cottonwood falls
we drank beer
out of my stetson
danced on brick streets
to bob wills
the texas swing
leaving my hat on
after too many longnecks
we made love
beside my old truck
like i was the last
cowboy on earth

cashed in her mfa

she wears plaid skirts
knee socks on saturday nights
drinks too much &
lets bald men spank her
for money &
tell her she's been a bad girl
but there's enough freaks
to pay the bills
put her kid through college
so she quit writing
poetry
a long time ago

on sundays she wears
fishnets to church
sits on the front pew
gives the preacher
a little hell fire
of his own
crosses & slowly uncrosses
her legs enough
that he yells
during the children's service

hallelujah
give me an amen

stays behind the pulpit

until way after

the sermon was over

haiku sonnet: child protective services

there isn't a blue
bird sitting on a cherry
tree blossom in march

that only happens in
photo shoots not here on dirt
roads with a single

wide trailers set back
in the woods trying to hide
the embarrassment

dad back in prison
mom strangled by meth
grandma too old/poor

a little girl sits at break-
fast counting her lucky charms

and those who can, teach

the six o'clock news
reported another school
incident, said a

young boy was hanging
out the elementary
school window holding

a sign that read *we*
love you written in
perfect cursive that

nobody teaches
anymore. the local law
called in the federal

bureau of investigation
for further analysis

johnny cash blues

i had a dream last night
that johnny cash and me
were kids together
before the black clothes
folsom prison blues
i walk the line
& martin guitars

we wore low top converse
and caught crawdads
out of the creek with paper clips
string and bacon
we smoked viceroys by the tracks

ya hear that train a comin
he whispered

i hung my head
and cried cause
the good dreams
never last long
enough

This project was made possible, in part, by generous support from the Osage Arts Community.

Osage Arts Community provides temporary time, space and support for the creation of new artistic works in a retreat format, serving creative people of all kinds — visual artists, composers, poets, fiction and nonfiction writers. Located on a 152-acre farm in an isolated rural mountainside setting in Central Missouri and bordered by ¾ of a mile of the Gasconade River, OAC provides residencies to those working alone, as well as welcoming collaborative teams, offering living space and workspace in a country environment to emerging and mid-career artists. For more information, visit us at www.osageac.org